Preserving Life through the Study of the Martial Way

Budo Taijutsu

Training Manual

Part One

By Professor Leon Drucker, Ph.D.

December, 2011

About the Author

Professor Drucker has been studying Martial Arts since 1964. He earned his Judo Black Belt in 1970 through his instructor, Legendary Judo Master Professor Takahiko Ishikawa.

His 48 plus years of experience includes training in Kodokan and Kosen Judo, Northern Shaolin Kung Fu, Yang Style Tai Chi Chuan. Professor Drucker's training also includes over 25 years of training in Kobujutsu and Budo Taijutsu. Professor Drucker has a PhD. in Nutrition and is a third generation-Massage Therapist and Holistic Health Practitioner. As a student of Anma Master Shogu Mochizuki, he refined his skills in the Traditional Art of Japanese Massage.

Professor Drucker has studied Yang Style Tai Chi Chuan since 1975 and considered a Master Teacher of Tai Chi Chuan. Professor Drucker is licensed to teach Bujinkan Ninpo Taijutsu, having personally received his Godan from Ninja Grandmaster Massasaki Hatsumi. Professor Drucker is one of only five instructors living in the United States considered Deshi or personal student of Kobujutsu Master Koryu Muramatsu and member of Myofu An Society of Japan.

Table of Contents

CHAPTER 1 - INTRODUCTION

CHAPTER 2 – COMBAT SPORTS VERSUS MARTIAL ARTS

CHAPTER 3 – THE EVOLUTION OF GRAPPLING ARTS

   Brief History of Grappling Arts

   Traditional Japanese Jujutsu

   Differences between Traditional Japanese Jujutsu and Modern Grappling

CHAPTER 4 – THE HEALING SIDE OF MARTIAL ARTS

CHAPTER 5 – PATH-NOTES

CHAPTER 6 – TECHNIQUE AND APPLICATION

CHAPTER 7 – POINTS OF STUDY

CHAPTER 8 - MYSTICISM

   Introduction

   Eastern

   Western

CHAPTER 9 – THE NATURAL WAY OF TAO

CHAPTER 10 – ZEN IN THE MARTIAL ARTS

   The Ten Ox-herding Pictures

CHAPTER 11 – MEDITATION FOR WARRIORS

CHAPTER 12 - CONCLUSION

REFERENCES

Chapter 1 - Introduction

Butterfly, these words
From my brush are not flowers,
Only their shadows

Soseki

The word Meijin is a person or expert that protects the life of nature by being a warrior. This book has been written in the hopes of bringing together these people who have the same goals of studying the natural world, and martial ways.

Just as in the origin of life, there are basic underlying principles that are the roots of Budo (*Martial Ways*). The martial way is to persevere, and so your heart must be immovable from the path, which leads to the foundation of peace. By not becoming a collector of technique, but rather allowing your self to become inspired and immersed in the study of Budo and by following an intuitive rhythm to natural fighting that comes through a calm presence of mind, you will come to understand these roots.

Budo Taijutsu literally means "Combat Body Skills," and takes into account the concept of Juppo Sessho no Jutsu, "contact in ten directions." Juppo Sessho is a vast idea that suggests a different mode of thinking and perception, including the ideas of foresight and perception. Other concepts such as Gogyo no Kata and San Shin, refer to the five elemental archetypes of Earth, Water, Fire, Wind, and Void. These concepts allow strategies to be applied to the way a particular technique or sequence might be influenced. To know these basic principles is more than just an academic or conscious understanding. You must have the ability to integrate these concepts through flashes of enlightenment during practice and meditation. Only then will you develop the basic feeling of actual fighting as well as the strategies needed in order to feel the real attitude of Budo Taijutsu.

Many books of knowledge train us to understand our position in the universe. In order to live by a code of morality these books provide us with rules and regulations restricting our bodily activities. We must learn to control our body so we can perfect our lives. Moreover, although these principles vary by country and time, the underlying regulations are the same. The duality that arises is that we live through our senses. We feel heat and cold, pleasure and pain because we identify with our bodies. All of us turn to material subjects for enjoyment and knowledge, but the eternal spiritual knowledge of which we really seek cannot be acquired through the body. The body in which we live is a result of the interaction of the modes of material nature, which is doomed to destruction from the moment it was made. We must learn to protect our body until we can transcend its conception of existence and attain our true nature.

This awareness of the true nature of our being is what enables the warrior to take the life of his opponent without any hesitation. Only by understanding the spiritual teachings can we hope to become true warriors and accept our own mortality in the face of death, unafraid, unflinching, or unwavering in our faith.

This book is not intended to be the final word on any of the topics included; it is merely an introduction of the concepts to encourage further study in any areas that interests the reader. There are vast numbers of books and other resources available in all areas of study of the martial way, which delve deeper on these specialties and subjects. The purpose of this book is to introduce the underlying areas usually reserved for the advanced initiate of Budo, rather than focus solely on the physical aspects. Many quotes from my personal teachers, as well as other research, books and authors have inspired me. I hope that I have not plagiarized their words but have interpreted them for the reader. I have compiled as complete a reference to these authors as I could for the reader to experience the depth of philosophy these masters have provided. This training manual is based on my own quest and discovery of this knowledge in hopes that the reader will find a commonality that will serve to encourage. I hope that this book will inspire you to enter or continue down the Warriors Path, to help preserve the Martial Way.

Chapter 2 – Combat Sports versus Martial Arts

Any book written about the martial arts since the advent of "Ultimate Fighting" should include at least a summary of the differences between the two. Many fans of Mixed Martial Arts (MMA) are under the illusion that since martial art is in the name and the combatants are fighting, as being sold to them by the promoters, that this is the modern equivalent of gladiator or at least as close to as you can get to real combat. The sad truth is that what makes for a very exciting sport, and in my opinion, probably the most demanding level of elite athlete the world has ever known, MMA as it is called, is the exact opposite of what real martial arts is all about.

Leave out the huge differences in rules and illegal technique deemed too dangerous for MMA. Just look at the internal aspects. It is readily apparent that MMA fighters are expected to dominate their opponent and beat them into submission. The martial artist seeks self control, mastery of thoughts and emotions, and wills himself to win with as little effort and exertion as possible. In combat martial arts, there are always risks as well as encouragement for the use of weapons. In combat sports, you are not allowed to kick someone in the groin or poke them in the eye without risk of disqualification. In traditional martial arts, there is generally more than one combatant in the arena of battle either as multiple attackers or in a battle with dozens, hundreds, and sometimes-even thousands of solders going on all at the same time within a limited space. In a world of rules, there are no rules. In controlled conditions such as clean and dry cushioned flooring, warmth and good lighting, in the art of war there are no such conditions and the warrior is battling the elements, hunger, overwhelming odds in both numbers and advantages of better fighting position. I hold no disrespect for the athletes of mixed martial arts or their fans. I am merely pointing out the obvious. MMA is a sport where you may be injured and at times quite seriously, but rarely risk death as in mortal combat. In reality, mortal combat is not about winning, being strong or fast. Rather it is about remaining in balance between the two extremes. It is about not being caught in a dualistic way of thought. If you focus on the vanity that goes along with being strong and winning you may forget that learning how to lose or even running away to remain alive is really the natural way to preserve life.

Now that I have pointed out some of the disparity between combat sports and martial arts what about the combatants and champions themselves. As a trainer, coach, and official for Ultimate Fighting, I do recognize certain similarities in professional fighters and warriors. Among the champion caliper fighters, there is a deep-seated character that separates them from most other men or women. It would only serve as a cliché to say that the best fighters come through enormous hardships and adversities. What is the difference between the elite athlete that has the ability to play baseball or football, which has huge financial rewards and someone willing to stand toe to toe in a cage and risk brain injury for a few thousand dollars? To spend months conditioning for an event that at most will be over within 20 to 25 minutes. The hundreds and even thousands of hours spent in the gym drilling technique and sparring, for only a few minutes of fame that sometimes is as fleeting as their next loss.

I do not wish to get into the intimate details of deviant behavior and will leave that for an author more versed in psychology. Nevertheless, I can tell you without a doubt that every fighter that I have ever known has some imbalance in their personality that allows for the years of suffering that they impose upon themselves in order to compete in Ultimate Fighting Combat Sports. For many men, the thought of rolling around on the ground shirtless or in spandex with another man is enough to stop any thoughts of training in this manner. For others the fear of being injured or the inability to deal with even the slightest pain prohibits this level of full contact sparring. So again, I ask the rhetorical question. What is it that would allow someone to go through the suffering of training, making weight, and the sacrifices needed to get ready for a fight? What is it that allows someone to take the risk of having an opponent's elbow or knee land on their face, the pain of joints being forced to bend in a direction that they are not intended to bend, or being choked unconscious? Unbelievably, that is not what the fighters think about. Losing is the hardest part of fighting. Motivating yourself to get back to training is extremely difficult after losing a fight. What shows the heart of these modern day gladiators? It is not the fear of injury; it is the fear of disappointing their family, friends, and fans. Is it the accolades of cheering fans with hands raised in honor of your latest conquest, or the fear of losing that motivates? Perhaps like everything else in life, in the end we all seek balance.

Chapter 3 – The Evolution of Grappling Arts

Brief History of Grappling Arts

One of the oldest forms of self-defense is the art of grappling. Records from ancient Egypt dating back almost 5400 years ago show images of grappling on tomb walls. The most famous styles of grappling arts were introduced in the Greek Olympic Games in 704 BC. This style of grappling was similar to modern Brazilian style Jujutsu. There were many other forms of grappling in the ancient world including, Pahalwani Mallayidya and Vajra Musti from India. From battlefields to self-defense and sport, wherever these styles came in contact with each other matches and technique spread all over the ancient world.

Sumo (Sumai, meaning struggle) matches were taking place in Japan Around 20 B.C. Chijura Kurabe was another grappling style that was be ing practiced, along with more battlefield styles such as Tekoi and Kumi Uchi. In addition, during this time, manipulation of the joints, as well as immobilization of the limbs (Yawara) were focused applications. Around 2800 years ago, Teijun Fujiwara developed what he called Aikijutsu. These techniques were derived from China and taught almost exclusively to the Japanese royal Minamoto family, where it remained a secret until the early 1100's. Although many styles of Jujutsu were developed over the centuries, most were associated with weapons. Using the strategy of yielding to an opponent's strength in order to unbalance and throw, Jujutsu involved a deep understanding the body. Jujutsu required an understanding of physiology and the dynamics of motion and forces to attack your opponent at his weakest point. Because this enables a weaker opponent to defeat a stronger one, Jujutsu became one of the fastest growing martial arts in the world.

In 1882, Jigoro Kano founded a new style of Jujutsu that he called Judo. Kano changed the philosophy of his art to appeal to the general public by removing many of the more deadly forms of Jujutsu techniques. The sporting and fitness aspects became the focus, and prearranged forms were taught for self-defense. These Kata ensured a safe learning environment and a way to rank students. Kano arraigned contests to test timing and technique in a semi-combat situation and targeted the school system as well as military and government officials. The popularity of Judo spread quickly and today is an Olympic sport practiced all over the world.

Japan was not the only country to develop modern versions of Jujutsu. In the 1920's V.A. Spiridonov studied European and Central Asian forms of grappling from Georga, Tadjik, Kasakh, Usbek, and Kirghiz. Combining the base elements, he founded Sambo (Russian form) in 1938. The Vikings and Norse practiced a grappling art called Glima over 1,000 years ago. Boke, the Mongolian name for wrestling was practiced in the 11th century in Inner and Outer Mongolia. The Naadam festival, (celebrating ?) is still held to this day every July. Another older form that has survived into the modern era comes from the Greek word for all-powerful, the Pankrateon style. The Greek hero of Attica, Theseus, founded Pankrateon, a grappling form that was introduced to the Olympic Games during the 33rd Olympiad. One of the oldest styles of Chinese Kung Fu, Shui Chao, is one of almost 60 different styles of grappling in China practiced 4000 years ago and still popular today. In Turkey, during the 1600's, grapplers were known for competing coated in oil, and securing leverage by grasping leather trousers or belts. Greco-Roman Wrestling originating from the 23rd Olympic Games is still practiced today; however, they are separated into two styles of grappling._Orthia pale or upright wrestling involved throwing your opponent to the ground, and Kato pale involved ground wrestling while coated in olive oil and then dusted with powder. In India, Kalari Payat was a very complete grappling system thousands of years ago which was introduced into Malaysia. The spread of grappling arts by the armies of Alexander the Great was another example of influence how these arts were interrelated. The most famous modern style of grappling is Brazilian Jujutsu founded by Helio Gracie. In 1915, Mitsuyo Maeda taught Judo to Carlos Gracie who then passed these techniques to his brother Helio. This form of Judo ground fighting was an extension of Kodokan as taught before World War II called Kosen Judo.

Traditional Japanese Jujutsu

There were many close-quarter combat systems developed in Japan for use by the Samurai. Jujutsu styles were to supplement the spear, sword, and archery when a weapon had been broken or lost in combat. Unarmed combat was only used as a last resort on the battlefield. Early forms of Jujutsu needed to take into account heavily armored combatants defending from possible weapons attacks. Classical Jujutsu emphasizes unarmed combat against multiple attackers. It also employed the use of various length swords, staffs, glaive, sickle & chain and spear. Grappling in armor was known as Yoroi Kumiuchi. This style focused on attacks to the portions of the body that the armor did not cover, as well as the use of the extra weight of the armor against the opponent.

Japanese Jujutsu training is done by way of Kata, which are pre-set forms involving two or more partners in various combative scenarios. The Kata was used to teach the various techniques and applications while developing the strategy needed for controlling timing and distance. These pre-set forms also developed physical and psychological attitudes for these otherwise lethal techniques, both unarmed and with weapons as full speed.

Differences between Traditional Japanese Jujutsu and Modern Grappling

Modern grappling is oriented towards gaining points or to submit your opponent in sanctioned and refereed matches. There are rules and the contest takes place on a mat with limited ring size. Since the contests are one on one, certain techniques are considered safe and even desirable such as working off your back to gain a submission rather than sweeping an opponent off you to get back to your feet. If you were grappling in a battlefield situation, the last thing a combatant would want is to be on his back any longer than to get up because of the threat from multiple armed attackers. In terms of strategy for Classical Jujutsu, any technique that makes it difficult to disengage from your opponent would be abandoned in place of a technique where the warrior could be ready in a split second to deal with a second or third attacker. The presence of weapons is another strategic consideration in Classical Jujutsu. This means there would be an emphasis on defense against grabs. The warrior would be trying to either draw their weapon or keep their opponent from drawing theirs.

Although there are many similar qualities and technique where the grappler would attack the joint, in Jujutsu there is more focus on pressure point as well as bone breaking, crushing muscle and putting an opponent on his back just long enough to draw a weapon and kill him. It is a big leap between threatening to tear ligaments and tendons and killing someone. If in a life or death situation, a wounded opponent may be even more dangerous. In classical Jujutsu, a finishing hold or submission is always followed by additional strikes to insure the opponent is no longer a threat. Limited mobility because of terrain, multiple combatants, and armor is another difference to consider when comparing modern sports grappling with classical Jujutsu. Submission grappling training consists of lots of free fighting along with individual situational drills. In classical Jujutsu, the techniques may be too lethal to practice in this manner, so it is rare to spar or do free fighting. Personally, I believe that there are many benefits gained from training in submission grappling. It is a complement to classical Jujutsu, and I find that students who cross train, progress faster and also develop a deeper understanding of Traditional Japanese Jujutsu.

The biggest problem with modern grappling is that the goal of individuals is based on dominating an opponent, rather than learning to control themselves. Rarely have I seen one of my grapplers cross over and become a student of Traditional Jujutsu. They are much too caught up in the competition and winning a match over their training partners and opponents. On the other hand, classical Jujutsu practitioners tend to be too caught up in their lineage and history of their martial arts. They are hesitant stepping out of their comfort zone and cross training in another school. Having a false sense of security and trust in their untested technique is another problem when practicing classical Jujutsu in a non-warring era. That is the reason modern competitive martial arts were developed in the first place. Students that include modern grappling with their traditional Jujutsu program will be able to have a realistic view of their limitations as well as strengths. It used to be very difficult to be accepted into a traditional school in ancient Japan, sometimes even requiring a student to sign a blood oath. Techniques were kept secret and only after many years would the student be allowed to learn the systems inner teachings. Today we have seminars, instructional DVDs, books, and the internet. I would encourage students of either modern grappling or traditional and classical Jujutsu to cross train and use all the resources available to them.

Chapter 4 – The Healing Side of Martial Arts

During my early years training with Professor Ishikawa, it was quite common for someone to get hurt during Randori (Free Fighting) which was done at every class as well as during our testing competition every 6 months. Since I was also competing in the Amateur Athletic Union (AAU), I was hurt occasionally during a throw or while ground fighting. Sensei would perform what he called Kappo (Resuscitation Techniques). There is a huge difference between being hurt during a match and an injury that is going to require a more prolonged therapy.

There are many old methods of traditional resuscitation, which can assist the victim in recovery. They have generally been replaced by CPR, which is based on more modern medical knowledge. Among sports coaches and medical professionals in the U.S., CPR is commonly recognized as the appropriate response to a medical emergency. Nevertheless, the traditional forms of resuscitation are considered advanced techniques of Jujutsu and instructors may wish to study them to complete their training for historical purposes or for use in special circumstances. Examples of these Kappo methods involve the direct massage of the carotid triangle on the neck to open up a collapsed artery. In addition, Kappo can manually stimulate the carotid sinus assisting the victim in waking up and focusing attention. Examples include slapping the victim, striking the sole of the foot, or yelling methods of inducing or simulating breathing. These methods include massage of the chest or diaphragm, to expand and contract the lungs. Three such methods of Kodokan Judo are Sasoi Katsu, the inductive method, Eri Katsu, the lapel method, and So Katsu, the composite method.

The Kodokan teaches Sasoi Katsu with the patient sitting before him. From behind, the practitioner bends his right knee and places the kneecap against the patient's spine. The practitioner then spreads his fingers, placing his hands on the patient's lower chest, he hooks his fingers under the lower ribs. Then pulling back as if opening the ribs to either side, he puts his weight on the shoulders to bend the body back, and presses with his right knee. This will draw air into the lungs. When the ribs have opened as far as they will go, release them. Air will be exhaled from the lungs. Repeat the process slowly and regularly. For traditional Eri Katsu, the practitioner kneels to the right of the victim and supports his upper body with the left arm around the shoulder. Putting the palm of his right hand on the abdomen, just above the navel, he presses up against the solar plexus or pit of the stomach. This will cause the diaphragm to rise, expelling air from the lungs. The practitioner reinforces the action by bending the upper body forward with your left arm and then gently releases the pressure to allow air to enter the lungs. This procedure is repeated until respiration is restored. For So Katsu lay, the victim on his or her back and kneel astride the hips. Place your hands, fingers spread apart and pointing toward his or her head, on the bottom of the rib cage. Lean forward and press against the ribs to make him or her exhale, and then relax the pressure. Repeat this procedure, rocking forward and back, until the victim can breathe without assistance. Similarly, this can be done with the victim on his stomach. In my professional career especially during the early years of mixed martial arts, there were many cuts, and eye injuries, which were less common in Randori practice and bouts.

The art of Anma is the foundation of all East Asian medicine and was brought to Japan in the 7th Century from China through Korea. Using no oil Anma involves stretching, squeezing and massaging to stimulate the body to become and or remain healthy. Anma focuses on improving muscle condition and the circulation of Ki, or Universal Life Energy. While Western massage techniques tend to focus on relaxing the client, the goals of Anma are to influence the internal organs, maintain balanced physical and psychological functioning of the body, reduce various ailments, and help with realigning of the physical structure. Anma is not Shiatsu, but Shiatsu is a part of Anma. It was not until 1964 that Shiatsu was recognized as distinct and independent from Anma massage. Originally, a Shiatsu therapist was a specialist who performed one Anma technique, the pressure method (Ap Paku Ho). Anma's foundation is the kneading technique, which combines with several different application techniques to construct the massage. The kneading technique (Ju Netsu Ho) and the percussion techniques (Ko Da Ho and Kyoku Te Ho) are a unique part of Anma and are not found in any other style of massage. There is a distinct cultural difference between the Eastern and Western view and values of health and health care. To practice Anma, it is important to understand the basics of how Asians view health and institutional health care. The point where illness is defined is substantially different. In the West, people tend to define illness through the diagnosis of a Western doctor/physician. A primary value in Asian culture is that good health and longevity are valued as the most important part of life, with prevention of disease at the foundation of it. In the West, treatment takes place upon the onset of severe symptoms, with little effort made at strengthening the body overall before disease sets in. The instant cure or rapid recovery is sought. There is also an over-reliance on doctors and other medical practitioners without much of an understanding that one must be responsible for his or her own health care. Westerners tend to view health as good, unless there are visible symptoms, and then it is bad. Everyone wishes their health to be perfect; being the ideal that only a few people are given. In East Asian people, there is no such thing as perfect health, because health is not perfect to start with. It is accepted that most people have some irregular or genetic defect of the human body. However, in East Asia trying to achieve balance is the objective, rather than striving for the unachievable perfect health. In the East, treatment takes place much earlier in the health care process, with East Asian medical providers looking towards prevention and early diagnosis as the measure of illness. Once noticeable symptoms appear, the illness is viewed as very advanced in Asian medicine. The objective of East Asian medicine is to try to diagnose in the early stages before symptoms appear. Treatment is much easier and recovery is quicker. As well, early detection prevents the spreading of illness.

Since Sensei Mochizuki has already written many wonderful books and continues to teach Anma. I will suggest that anyone interested more on this subject contact Master Mochizuki for class schedules and training locations. Doctor Mochizuki has helped teach me to balance the ability to injure someone with the ability to help facilitate health. The Yin and Yang or In and Yo depending on the language, seems to be a consistent progress as one becomes more advanced in their martial prowess and maturity. Almost every single martial arts master that I know also happens to be a very talented and advanced practitioner of some form of medicine. You cannot be a complete master of the martial arts without balance so it only makes sense that if you can hurt someone you should also be able to help them recover.

Chapter 5 – Path-notes

One of the conflicts that arise in taking the martial path is that at some point there is realization and even an impulse to shrink from the violence we see in the human condition. Although we are trained to perform violence when required and confront death in order to transcend the limits of worldly existence there is a dramatic moral crisis that is central to developing the faith needed to perform our sacred duty. A paradox interconnects disciplined action and freedom. We must explore within ourselves concepts such as duty, discipline, action, and knowledge to allow for our ultimate understanding of phenomenal existence. Our freedom lies in disciplined action that is both performed without attachment to the action itself while being dedicated with loving devotion to those we hold dear. How can we continue to act in a world of pain without suffering and despair and enable ourselves as warriors to control our passion and become men of discipline? The real battlefield is the human body, where within this material realm we struggle to know oneself.

As I have matured and developed, the violence, which can occur during practice, has all but disappeared. When I was a young student, we would pride ourselves on the intensity of our practice showing off bruises, cuts, and injuries as badges of honor. Now I feel compassion for my Uki (attacking training partner). I do not want to hurt them during demonstration of form or technique. You do however; learn a lot being used as a crash test dummy by your sensei. Try to insure a safe if not entirely pain free experience if possible. Grow less and less attached to technique that requires control of an attacker with pain by way of a series of strikes, throws, joint manipulations and pain. Most beginning students training to learn the martial arts are interested in the way to protect themselves from threat or attack. Teach them how to be kind to each other, and how to be compassionate, caring people. New students expect technique; advanced students should grow less attached to form. Literally having no idea of what is going to happen, have your Uki attack with a punch, kick or throw. Surrender to an attack, but do not allow Atemi (striking) to land. Find yourself moving from neutral to neutral without any emotion or attachment to doing anything other than avoidance. At some point, the opening will be there. Decide to end their attack as simply as possible. Allow the accident to happen. Beginning students first learn to paint by number. Then they are encouraged to find their own way and allowed the options of adapting the technique based on their build, limitations, experience, and training partner. Make up your own ending as long as you adhere to the basic concept. I encourage my students to play as I hear the echo of my own teachers. Sensei, should I do the technique this way? Yes, case by case.

Make sure that you practice solid fundamentals even if studying advanced concepts. Allow the development of your own eclectic style combining your experience and the best qualities of your own teachers. Reflect on your insights of the techniques in order to understand the deeper meaning of what is being practiced. Am I actually doing anyone any favors by providing a distillation of years of practice and reflection saving you the enormous sacrifice that I have made in my own life in order to learn and integrate these lessons. Am I depriving you of your own personal discoveries by spoon-feeding? My desire to communicate verbally may save you a little work and sacrifice, but by no means replace putting in the effort to learn for yourselves. I have learned to be encouraging and try to be patient. The way is the way and must unfold much like a mythic quest.

We can produce a sword that is capable of cutting but far from a work of art. The student will determine whether function is more important than form as you see that a very sharp sword, in the hands of someone unable to cut properly is still very dangerous. Hesitation from lack of confidence could cost you your life, if you are not capable of entering under the blade you will be the one cut down. I see my students' lack of dedication, and understand that they may never come to a deep level or mastery of the art. It is far easier to develop an academic understanding of the area of study than learning to apply that knowledge. My father many times has told me that the wise man knows where to find the answer. In Budo, there is no one answer because there is no one way. We cannot guess what someone is going to do in a fight. Because we have memorized a technique or can go look it up in our notes understand and apply what is appropriate. You get what you are capable of getting. You get what you are looking for. You get what you put into it. In the larger scope, it really does not matter. Learning Budo is an individual process, which can involve group dynamics within the Dojo (school) but ultimately is deeply personal.

Some people enter the Dojo empty allowing me to fill their cup; others whose cups are full can still have fun. Either way we can enjoy our time together. I can stop worrying about making it too easy or extremely hard for my students. I realize that this is really just part of my own quest anyway. I will share what I can, giving the student some ideas to contemplate. I can help to motivate them and encourage them to work hard. Yet, in the end, my words are meaningless as wind in dry grass. Some are capable of hearing the rhythm and not fixate on the notes, of seeing the spaces between and enjoying the time of being present, others collect and are never present. There is no need to memorize the song, but why even listen if you cannot relax and enjoy the process? We have all heard ourselves humming a tune and wondered where we have heard it. Technique when applied correctly is just like that forgotten tune. We can chose to make an accident happen, but when the accident just happens, that truly is the highest level of skill expressed in martial arts.

For most of us, we live a life of frustration, anxiety, agitation, and addiction. Sometimes it just feels so futile and meaningless. Our brief years of life are filled with difficulties due to circumstances of war, pestilence, famine and many other disturbances. We want a high standard of living within a complex stimulation of the senses, which ultimately makes us less sensitive and in need of even more violent stimulation. We crave distractions of sights and sounds, of thrills crowded into the shortest possible time. We live lives that consist of doing jobs that are boring in order to earn a means to seek relief from our hectic and expensive pleasures. We justify our lives so that we may rear a family because we do not know what else to do. We either have faith that there is a life after death or feel that the whole thing is so futile that we spend our whole life pretending that it is not. I am not making any secret claims to some mysterious knowledge. Like you, I am trying to understand the great mystery of why I am here and have chosen a path that seems to suit my personality, and gives me hope that there is a reason to it all.

At times of expanded consciousness, I understood that I am a perfect spiritual being living in a body of meat. I am not only attached, but also very dependent on this body for the time being. My reasons for getting involved with martial arts, was for the most part an effort to remove fear from my life. Later on the reasons changed as I matured and noticed an underlying pattern that transcended style, label and physical attributes which has kept me going along the path towards protecting the body I have become so dependent on. The Dojo is a place where I can help others motivated by the same concerns for themselves and their families.

When I first started teaching, I would ask new students why they wanted to study the martial arts. Most of the time their reasons were to attain "Black Belt", and someday have their own school, which was a level of expertise they could measure as well as a stroking of ego. Those same students after a very short time changed the reasons to things like, I enjoy class, I have fun here, or I have made many new friends. What I noticed was that those students had lost their fear of being attacked and not knowing what to do. They had gained an improvement of balance not only within the dojo but within their own lives as well. In addition, they now came to an understanding that some things can never be perfected. In a world where we are always trying to get from point A to point B as quickly as possible, we have forgotten how to be present. I have discovered that when I stop living in the past or visualizing the future not only am I happier but also have a whole lot more energy at my disposal. Aside from that, why rush through life when this may be our one chance to see it all. This is my own reason for continued practice after 47 years. I know that the universe is a process, which is also within me. The problems arise when I chose to ignore this process.

Chapter 6– Technique and Application

An application is the transition between Kamae (stance) that links a variety of movements, which are labeled as a technique. These techniques are arranged in conditional sequences for the purpose of training and are called Kata. When practicing Budo, Kata is one of the tools we use, but in doing Budo, the Kata must be forgotten. To use another analogy think about someone playing the piano. First, they must learn the names and location of the notes. The student then practices playing scales to become familiar with sequence and start the process of seamlessly playing a song by either ear or written score. Early on, feeling is not as important as losing the awareness that you are actually looking at, or remembering the song and not feeling the process involved. If a musician is too much in their head, they become aware of reading. They will feel their fingers pressing on each key. If you are worried about playing the song correctly as taught, you will never get to the next step. A musician must add feeling to the song, owning it and communicating this emotion.

Because of our martial heritage, the techniques and applications have already been set down for us by the great masters of the past. We do not need to reinvent the wheel, only discover how to use the wheel for ourselves. Striking can be done with many parts of the body from the head to the toes. Whether we are kicking, punching, or chopping, the movement includes borrowed power from our opponent plus issued power starting from the ground transmitted through our body. Proper striking requires that our posture allow for a stacking of bones so we do not rely on muscle power and an acceleration of inertia as we accelerate through our target to maximize the force. Depending on the strike, there is a sequence that must happen. Starting with letting go and allowing the strike to happen; we must also be shifting our weight, turning our waist and feet as if we were throwing, whipping, or shaking.

With beginning students of martial arts, they are usually concerned with punching and kicking harder. As the student progresses they realize that just like chopping down a tree, striking is an accumulation of applications that allow for the finalizing action. One of the applications that must be understood is compression. This occurs when we strike someone in a way that causes him or her to root, which allows the target to stop moving away. This is related to loading up a leg by pulling down on the Gi before a throw. One of the best ways to compress someone is a focused strike to pressure points as taught in Koshijutsu. As an example, picture a thumb strike or boshiken to the side of the neck just under the ear. A typical reaction is the raising of the shoulders and leaning away from the poke. This is compression and allows the finalizing strike to drop or knock out our opponent. Another name for compression is sealing and if you have ever had the wind knocked out of you then you are familiar with sealing the breath.

One of the most advanced concepts in martial arts is Koppojutsu. Koppo sometimes referred to as bone breaking art but in reality, it is the way of unbalancing by displacing the bones. When I think of Koppo, I think about multiple bouncing strikes that cave a person down on themselves like one of those toys where you press on the bottom and it just collapses on itself. As you strike, the body reacts to the strike, bouncing naturally to the next target and so on, accumulating many small strikes, which will again, in the tree analogy allow it to fall. In my class I have several students who are at least a foot and half taller than I am. By first striking their legs or floating rib, I can always bring their head down to a level where it then makes sense to hit there. There is also something much deeper going on when you start to collapse someone with Koppojutsu. As the body bends, it compresses nerves that branch out from the spinal cord through the spine out to the limbs. As the neck bends, it compresses on nerves feeding the arms and makes them weaker, much easier to manipulate, so even if planning on a joint reversal a good way of entering is with Koppo or Koshijutsu (finger bone art). At the very least, a well-placed punch to the inside of the shoulder will weaken any incoming or possible strike from that arm for several seconds. Bouncing off the shoulder up under the jaw will force the head back and compress the cervical vertebrae possibly keeping that person from stepping backward and allowing a kick to the inside hip causing rotation. The progressive sequence of strikes will topple even the most solid and formidable oaks in the forest.

Do not use strength. If strength is used then the back and neck will be stiff and no energy will flow to the top of the head. If the energy does not flow and the blood does not circulate freely then the spirit cannot rise up. Using strength allows you to easily be manipulated. Use your mind instead of strength. If you can relax the whole body it will help you to avoid being clumsy. Being relaxed also allows the unrestricted flow of blood and energy. By using mind instead of strength, we can rely on the connective tissues allowing our movement to be more light, circular, and spontaneous.

Avoid expanding the chest. If you expand the chest then energy will be held in the upper body and cause you to be top heavy. Allow the back to raise and that is where you will issue power. When you avoid expanding the chest then you can sink your weight lowering your center of gravity.

Relax the waist. The waist is one of the most vital areas. If power is lacking, look to the cause, which is usually waist movement. Once the waist is relaxed, you can have a strong foundation but the feet will still be able to move. Relax your shoulders and keep your elbows down. This will allow you to relax your whole body. By relaxing, we can deliver much more force in our sticking. This may be one of the most difficult things to accomplish especially in during a fight. Relaxation requires release of all tension. Try to feel the difference between full and empty. Do not allow all the weight to rest on one leg. Being double weighted also keeps you from being light, nimble, and natural rather than heavy and stiff. This principle is very important for balance.

Unify the entire body. As taught by Master Yang Cheng Fu, "The root is in the feet; it is issued through the legs, controlled by the waist, and expressed in the hands." There must be a continuous flow of energy throughout the entire body along with a synchronized movement. This unification is also of the body, mind, and spirit. Allow the spirit to command the body by raising the spirit and opening the mind. Every movement should be complete, continuous, and circular.

Find the stillness in movement. Be patient, slow down, and allow the breath to be long and deep. There is a quiet place we enter when we surrender. Time slows down and allows you to see what your opponent is about to do or is doing. It is this stillness in the movement that allows us to have grace. When we move, our posture should be balanced, upright, uniform, and even. Stick and follow as a conscious movement by forgetting yourself and not separating from your opponent but rather joining with him.

Remember that energy and force are not the same. Energy comes from the connective tissue and force from the bones. Energy is a property of being soft, flexible, and alive. Force is a property of hard and inflexible. Learn to distinguish the difference. When you issue energy, it should be like shooting an arrow. The arrow relies on the elasticity of the bow and string, which allows delivery of power. Also, understand the difference between pulling and repelling. When you pull, it should be in the direction of force, and when you repel it should start with the following of energy and then a deflection. Do not use your own force but borrow it from your attacker. If you add too much force, you will be unable to escape or release and it will give your opponent momentum to pull you with him.

A dynamic flexibility creates unitary power by not focusing on relaxed flexibility. Rather focus on specific points that are not relaxed for greater extension alone. These points can be connective or bone structures that improve extension and power. We are not stretching but strengthening the bodies springing power. Being relaxed and loose does not mean feeling weak. It means that the body can have proper alignment and stability. Once we are relaxed, the energy, which is inherent to the body, can be utilized. Depending on varying degrees of consciousness, mental focus, and efficiency, while using the principles of physics, this energy helps us apply proper issuing of both muscle and mind power.

Other methods of delivering power require a compression or storage of energy. By having strong ligaments and the ability to focus using proper strategy, timing and advantageous positioning we can compress and release like a spring. We can also store energy by twisting to create a more penetrating strike as we drill or unwind. There is also a wave like method that is also loose and springy. You can compare this energy to the way a wave moves through a whip to its tip. Understanding and the use of these energies are two different things and we gain proficiency only after much perseverance and practice. Through perseverance and practice, we can awaken qualities without intellectual pursuit. A few of these goals can be patience, attention, endurance, stamina, ease, and will power. Budo is a synthesis of opposites as well as of similarities. Just like finding the stillness in activity, we seek a state of being and becoming. We quiet our mind to be more alert and allow no distinction between transient, flowing, or arrested time.

Whole body power occurs when the body acts as a single unit. By delivering your strike through the waist, you can accelerate movement. In addition, you should use the weight of your body. This movement is a pouncing action coming through the hips. When all the muscles of the body work together in harmony there is an internal opposing power that develops similar to the action of drawing a bow. In other words, when the whole body is used, the power generated is a release of the opposing power of the muscles. By adding continuity, you can then follow your opponent's movement and continue attacking. You never stop changing and redirecting his power. Think about a tiger who pounces and misses, he will pounce again and again, so the pray cannot get away. You must not only understand the martial technique, but also only by employing these qualities will you master Budo.

Our training must strengthen the connective tissue, the muscles and the body. What good is all the other more esoteric training without a strong body able to withstand blows, as well as issue all the power you have learned how to develop? So have a good bumper as well as a good engine. Your engine will allow you to keep up with your opponent even if nothing else is working. By training your forms or Kata as well as the basics you can strengthen the body as a bumper and develop the energy needed to fuel your engine.

Be heavy when you engage or when someone contacts you. Employ spring and shaking exploding natural power when you strike. Think about how a dog shakes water off instead of just striking. Do not lose your opponent when they change direction. Even if you knock them down you must stick with them not just watch. You must make your body a part of their body. Be loose not stiff while being heavy. Make sure that all parts of the body are interlocked to become one unit and spiral your movement. Work on increasing your range of motion to allow for extension of the joints. This will keep the weight out of the knees and into the hips. Do not be afraid of experimenting with the movements to make them your own. Also, keep in mind that once you start thinking about what technique you are going to do, your opponent can sense this. So let your body work by itself. If you do not know what you are doing than neither can your opponent. To apply these same ideas to your teaching requires you to stop trying to teach. Instead, show a natural way of movement, which your students can, then steal for themselves. Manipulate the perceptions of truth and falsehood in order to deceive an opponent. You must force your opponent to draw false conclusions, so that instead of knocking them down you can let them fall down for you. Appearances are deceptive so be aware that when you think there is nothing there is always something.

Chapter 7 – Points of Study

For most beginning students of martial arts, you start with learning various postures or Kamae and forms or Kata. Later on come drills for practicing technique. In grappling arts, most new students spend a lot of time learning Ukemi (receiving). Ukemi is usually interpreted as a rudimentary level of breakfalls and rolling in order to avoid getting hurt, while practicing throws and other technique that includes takedowns. Hidden within these basic skills are the layers of the deeper levels and understanding to the fundamentals of Budo. Devoting your training to perfecting technique can lead to a set way of thinking and responding. Once you are predictable, your opponent can make use of this. Of course as a beginner, it is necessary to learn Kata and technique so you can absorb the concepts and begin to catch the feeling of Budo. Eventually you will need to destroy all forms, which have become fixed habits.

Kamae is not just a posture to move to and from but more importantly a manifestation of mental and spiritual power. There is intention and energy that is projected naturally. Part of the process of mastering Kamae is first to feel this natural projection, then to intensify and finally to hide or give a false sense. It is extremely dangerous in the world of real martial arts for your opponent, to immediately and clearly see what your intentions are. For a trained fighter this is what exposes the weak points. To understand each Kamae takes time to settle into the frame, to not only study the posture and the way your body feels but to reflect on the reason we move into and out of each frame while practicing Kata. When first learning Kamae, hold the posture upwards of 12 to 15 minutes in order feel the weakness in your body. Study what muscles are being strained, what corrections are needed to correct posture and poor balance. Can you move easily into another Kamae? How must you shift weight in order to move smoothly? These questions you must ask yourself first. After 30 minutes, you are able to perceive natural intention. Before deep understanding of Kamae, your martial arts will have no spirit.

Students of Budo should take detailed notes. Describing the movement from Kamae to Kamae is a good way of explaining the physical and emotional aspects of a Kata. By minimizing the description of the movements to the basics such as: starting with left foot forward in Seigan no Kamae step out and back slightly with the right foot to Kosei no Kamae while blocking the attackers right punch with your left elbow to the inside of their right elbow. Step forward with right foot into Ichimonji no Kamae while executing a right Shuto to the left side of their neck. After this type of brief description may come some small notes such as not banging knees, angle of attack, leaning forward and allowing the left leg to rotate and counterbalance the counterstrike, be aware of possible left punch counter etc, etc. Then the important points can be added such as how the attack made you feel, what possible variations came up, what type of mistakes you should watch out for. Perhaps you were training with someone that was a foot taller and a hundred pounds heavier than you were while learning the technique. You might want to add something about the difficulties you encountered. Later on when reviewing your notes, you may want to add how to use these similar tactics in an interpersonal confrontation using words instead of fists. Perhaps you could think how Kata could be used in dealing with a problem at work or with another sport or activity. The biggest danger lies when you start to collect Kata ignoring that they are only a way of teaching. Kata is not something to be memorized and used as an application to a specific attack. In a fight, there is not time to think or remember what to do. Your body reacts naturally from thousands of hours of practice. Notebooks are for reference to review while practicing and years later to help when you may have forgotten a particular technique.

Attempt to learn how to build a beautiful cabinet, not to be the master of hammer and nail. Distance and timing, while wrapping your opponent up in space with nothing to cling to, is just as important as moving freely. You should not worry about making mistakes while training but rather develop a flexible frame of mind, which will allow you to flow into a fresh solution. Trying to win, using power and being set in your ways in a real fight will get you killed. Not only do our thoughts influence our bodies but also it is also true that our bodies influence our thoughts. Do not try to fit a situation into a pre-set plan, rather adapt to your surroundings. Once you stop thinking about individual technique and start flowing, there will be no fixed point for your opponent to attack.

You must pace yourself while training Kata being careful not to rush. The speed will be there when you need it, but it is much more important to break things down so your flow does not leave openings. When training with a partner try to match their speed and not react too quickly. Allow time to see where your partner is going. Only move quickly when you finish technique.

Sanshin literally means three hearts; it is practical martial study that enables the martial artist to learn the integration of body, mind, and spirit. Sanshin allows the student to examine the elemental archetypes of earth, water, fire, wind, and void, and to study the human forms of these archetypes as seen in personality types. The concept can be understood in its most basic terms. Religion has simplified everything into good and evil. Instead of good and evil, suppose we were to look at positive and negative? Segmenting a masculine and feminine form, we can now look at one of these elements as an example that can explain the concept.

Every one of us has met an example of a man who has had the personality of the element earth. What would that person be like? Let us say this person is a positive manifestation of masculine earth. Their personality would be supportive, someone whom you could rely on. If they were a negative manifestation of masculine earth, you can see how this person would be viewed as stubborn or unchanging. Aside from physical attributes such as size, we are looking at personality and a way they would react to any number of situations. How would we deal with someone unyielding and stubborn in his or her thinking and movement? Perhaps if we were physically stronger and larger or even more unyielding we could have a shoving match emotionally, either verbally or physically. Unfortunately, this type of thinking usually has a winner and a loser. The weaker opponent would lose the battle. However, if we were to have an understanding and ability to understand the personality in terms of elemental archetype there would be a strategy. Furthermore, we could choose the appropriate element to neutralize, defuse, or remove any potential conflict. There would not be a winner or loser. There would be no disadvantage to physical or mental strength, or even will power. When you know others there is wisdom, but to master them requires force. Rather than force use your inner strength and master yourself. If you can learn to sense, and project an archetype devoid of emotion, again using the words of Lao Tzu, the rhinoceros can find no place to thrust their horn, the tiger no place to use their claws and no weapon a place to pierce. As the ancients say, Yield and overcome." (Lao Tsu)

The studies of these elements are vital strategies to understanding the proper attitude when approaching any manner of situation. When you practice keep in mind that there is intention behind every action. There is the intention of your opponent as well as yourself. There is also a universal intention that you have no control over other than to surrender. Understanding universal intention and your place within this great mystery allows for the beginning of integration of San Shin. We can train our bodies, mind and spirit, but to what purpose? How do we integrate the three hearts? Is it because we want to dominate another to our will, or serve a universal intention, to which we were born onto this earth? Through the study of Sanshin, you will come to understand emotional growth.

In order to apply technique correctly there are many points of study, which are actually much more important to understand. In fact, the technique is only another form or frame with which we can study the application of these concepts. Although many metaphors transcend the physical, it is a primary way that we can communicate and come to understand and transfer knowledge. For example, when we speak about flexibility most beginning students of the martial arts may think the reference is to the body only. Flexibility in thinking may be more practical in aiding someone to flow then a limber body. A foundation is critical, but to deviate from the foundation or form is art. Through the practice of technique and the proper understanding of the application, we ultimately learn how technique is developed from the fundamentals. It should be the ultimate goal of any martial artist to forget technique after it has served its purpose of exposing and allowing the practice of the fundamentals such as listening with the body. Following your opponent's movement by sticking to ultimately leads to the application of technique. These concepts are difficult to explain without metaphor, technique, and forms training. The transmission of this knowledge is non-verbal and so almost impossible to describe without a reference point.

In Zen, the process teaches, not in words but direct pointing or engaging in a game with ourselves in which the only answer is a new level of consciousness. Therefore, just as in Zen, martial arts training is a game of insight where we can discover who we are underneath the masks and roles that we call personality as well as finding our way to the core principles.

As a student of Budo, one can chose to just memorize technique or find the source. Understanding the source is the difference between being and artist or painting by the numbers. Both will get you a nice picture to look at but in Budo could get you killed. I am talking about the deconstruction of technique rather than the focus. In order to build new mental pathways we must practice form. We learn concentration and awareness as we become conscious of our physical transformation. One of the core areas of study is the concept of Juppo Sessho.

Instead of isolating all the points of study, I would prefer to explain the integration of a collective of ideas that include core principles such as Koteki Ryoda to facilitate transformation. Movement, like good calligraphy, should continue with the mind. We do not overextend our body but as we regain balance, we must also be concerned with momentum of the body, mind, and spirit. Being rooted can be a good place to strike from but can lead to an inability of flow. So how do we balance and root while sticking and following? How do we find the tempo so we may change the timing to leading by following? Ko means tiger and Ryo means dragon. In some ways, this term means combining the physical power of the tiger, which is known for its powers of prediction and hunting prowess along with the non-physical or spiritual world of the dragon. We have an image of these two worlds coming together as the world in which we live and the world that permeates us. If you look at Koteki as the way a tiger strikes with total abandonment living in the moment, and Ryoda as the dragon capture. This combination is a method of interchange between two realms, as the battle that exists within us all of truth and falsehood.

As we follow our opponent's energy, we must find a way to neutralize or deflect then change or reverse their attack. We do this with the 10 keys of control. Most people think of physical direction. There is up and down, left and right or any angle in between as well as forward and backward. If we add in the dimensions of space / time, and creation through intention, we approach a level of control of any situation that transcends blocking, punching and kicking to rudimentary and vulgar forms of interaction. Juppo Sessho is a means of training our awareness to be everywhere, linking our physical body to the universe. We must first receive our attack from a neutral place of no mind. Being soft, we adhere to our opponents raising energy with automatic motion and peripheral awareness. We relax and allow our waist to turn, our joints to sink and a unity to form. As we follow the intention of our attacker, we appear and disappear with artistry and precision, stepping consciously with peaceful or wrathful gaze. By borrowing and sinking, we momentarily root to deliver power of central equilibrium. Using the energies of spiraling and explosive force we uproot and open, we split and we interrupt. The transference of power is only after drawing in your opponent both mentally and physically, borrowing their strength and as if shooting an arrow or like a dog shaking water, strike, throw, or cut, case by case.

Chapter 8 - Mysticism

Introduction

"Who am I and why am I here?" Man has asked these questions since he first became conscious. The connection between the Occult Sciences or Mysticism and Martial Arts varies depending on the country of origin and era in which we use as a reference. Western science is just now beginning to understand the realm of mind and matter because of the latest research into particle physics and advances in technology allowing us to explore the vast unseen world of what the universe, time space and reality is really comprised of, and how it all works. Underlying all mysticism is an elaborate symbolism used to illustrate and explain the cosmos. So rather than create the massive work required to explore this topic in the context of location and history I would like to briefly touch on the fundamental teachings in summary.

Eastern

If we look at ancient Hindu and Buddhist cosmography as explained by experts in the occult sciences of India and Tibet there are many manuscripts that talk of reality and can be summarized in the following fundamental teachings.

All conditions, or realms of existence such as worlds, heaven or hell are entirely dependent upon phenomena. This phenomenon is not only transitory but also illusionary and unreal except in the mind perceiving them. In reality, there are no beings anywhere such as gods, demons, spirits, or even people, just phenomena dependent on a cause. This cause is the yearning after sensation by the unstable existence of a cosmic consciousness. Only by overcoming the attachment to sensation, can we become enlightened and get off the wheel of birth and death. Death itself is nothing more than a continuation under changed conditions of the phenomena born existence of the human world. The nature of existence that governs this cycle of death and rebirth even in the state between these two realms is Karma determined by the actions we take and perhaps even our thoughts. After death, we enter a prolonged dream state filled with illusions that directly result from our mental content. Only by realizing that our existence is an illusion can we become enlightened and become emancipated from the cycle and enter Nirvana a state beyond existence. As was spoken by the Buddha himself to his disciples (Lecture of the Noble Eight Fold Path):

> "There is a realm devoid of earth and water, fire and air. It is not endless space, nor infinite thought, nor nothingness, neither ideas nor non-ideas. Not this world nor that is it. I call it neither a coming nor a departing, nor a standing still, nor death, nor birth; it is without a basis, progress, or a stay; it is the ending of sorrow. For that which clingeth to another thing there is a fall; but unto that which clingeth no fall can come. Where no fall cometh, there is rest, and where rest is, there is no keen desire. Where keen desire is not, naught cometh or goeth; and where naught cometh or goeth there is no death, no birth. Where there is neither death nor birth, there neither is this world nor that, nor in between, it is the ending of sorrow. There is and unbecome, unborn, unmade, unformed; if there were not this unbecome, unborn, unmade, unformed, there would be no way out for that which is become, born, made, and formed; but since there is and unbecome, unborn, unmade, unformed, there is escape for that which is become, born, made and formed."

Western

With its roots in the ancient Egyptian occult, intertwined with the social history of Europe, the Kabbalah is not only central to understanding the spirituality of Judaism but also Western mysticism. The main teachings are that we once lived in communion with God but were cast out of this garden of paradise and yearn to return. There is a map, which is called the "Tree of Life." This map symbolizes the different levels that we must pass through to get back to the garden. The symbolism gives us insight into not only our psychological world and how our minds work but also reveals the essence of our spiritual existence as well.

Just as in Eastern mysticism, the Kabbalah explains how God (ourselves) moves out of this place of nonexistence in order to experience, and gives rules of conduct and a path back to cosmic consciousness and oneness with all. This path, the Tree of Life, expresses ten archetypal levels. These levels are the Crown, which could be likened to God.

1) Wisdom, which represents a place where God can experience him/herself;
2) Understanding, where God finds the limits of experience;
3) Mercy, where we find the qualities of helping others;
4) Severity, which gives us the strength to face what is wrong and try to change them similar to what the term Karma refers to in Eastern traditions;
5) Balance, representing the core of most schools of martial arts;
6) Understanding, on many levels, the difference between pride and ego and the higher self;
7) Passion, represents the creative process both in man and nature;
8) Thought, the illumination of the unconscious mind;
9) Feeling, which corresponds to the physical body and the application of energy;
10) The Body itself which is comprised of the elements of Earth, Water, Air and Fire symbolically making up all matter.

The rules of conduct, being central to any esoteric tradition, allow some form of reinforcement in developing an egoless behavior. An example of these attributes by one of the brilliant teachers Moses Cordovero is as follows: Forbearance in the face of insult, and patience enduring evil. Pardon or erase any evil suffered, and identify with your neighbor. He also stresses complete absence of anger, combined with appropriate action as well as mercy, to the point of recalling only the good qualities of your tormentor. You must eliminate all traces of vengefulness and forget any suffering inflicted on you by others while trying to remember only the good.

Central to all religions, are spiritualism and mysticism, along with the concept of Compassion for the suffering of others without judging. Cordovero prays for the attributes of truthfulness and mercy even beyond the letter of the law. He asserts that assisting the wicked to improve without judging them and remembering that all human beings are innocent of their infancy, are both important qualities. By embodying these divine qualities beyond their usual human limits, the mystic sought to become a pure vessel ready for the higher knowledge, contemplation, and honor of God's creation.

Chapter 9 – The Natural Way of Tao

For us to achieve and live in a way that is neither passive or of constant struggle we must learn the ways of the Taoist. Taoism was brought forth five hundred years before Christ in a book entitled, "Tao Te Ching," by Lao Tsu. This book formed the foundation of Taoism with four basic tenants. The Tao, (way) underlies all things; human action is harmonious, effortless and spontaneous as well as inexhaustible; when perfected the individual is free from desire; and should help guide all people and governments back to a state of harmony with Tao.

Even thought we cannot really explain the Tao we are capable of living it. If we are able to forgive ourselves for mistakes and stop blaming others for our wounds either emotional or physical, even in our ignorance of the Tao we can live a life in harmony with nature. When we separate living in harmony with nature and the human spirit we lose touch with our feelings and our thoughts become relative and subjective. If we can follow a life where we live in harmony with our spirit and the natural world, then intuition and feelings guide us to visions and insight of the truth and essence of the Tao.

It is unfortunate that in this world of technology our culture has lost the way of nature. We must reunite with the earth as a living being "Gaia," and stop thinking of it as something to be exploited. Only then can we begin to find our way back from this separation of thinking of ourselves as separate from nature. There are many theologies and teachings that can help guide us back to the unification of nature and spirit. There is a rebirth of holistic thinking, which allows us to create new forms of education and inspire more ecological economies, agriculture, and government. The Tao cannot be lost because it is the way of wisdom and eternal truth.

The essence of Taoism contained within the "Tao Te Ching," is comprised of eighty-one chapters, which for the last 2,500 years provided and influenced Chinese culture and thought with the proverbs of Lao Tsu. Without attempting to interpret, I would like to briefly summarize these proverbs in a language that most of us will understand. Many scholars have spent a lifetime studying this book, as well as wonderful organizations dedicated to spreading the word of Taoism that would be a much better source of information should you chose to learn more. To those teachers I apologize if my attempt falls short or you feel my summary is inaccurate. I am a student seeking to encourage others to read the proverbs for themselves not replace or interpret this beautiful and timeless work of art.

The way that can be told is not the way.
The way is just a path to be followed and it can never be used up.

We can see beauty only because there is ugliness and good because there is evil.

Try to lose your desire of things external.

People appear ignorant to nature so stick to the middle, more is less.

Nature is our mother and will never fail to provide.
Nature lasts forever because it is unborn.

Water provides us with an example of the way because if flows everywhere.

Do not overdo things.

Avoid separation of spirit and nature just as you were when born.

Be understanding and nourish without taking credit, do not try to dominate.

It is the spaces between that are useful to show us what is there.

Be guided by what you feel not what you see, do not always trust your senses.

The human condition is difficult so just accept it.

Try to care for all things as if they were your own.

The Tao cannot be seen, heard or felt, it is formless without a beginning or end.

Stay in the present.

Sometimes we cannot understand something but only the appearance can be described.

Try not to seek fulfillment or desire for things to change.

Empty yourself and let your mind rest at peace.

If you do not allow yourself to trust then how can you expect someone to trust you?

When there are problems in society or within a family or country, someone will come along who will have the pretense of wisdom and devotion to help. Be aware that their morality and kindness should be questioned.

Being simple, without being selfish nor desire for profit and no one will try to steal from you. It is not enough to only have what you need, give up everything and surrender so that nature can take care of you.

If you follow the one path and trust even though you cannot see where it leads, your faith will show you the way to creation.

Yield to overcome.

Nothing lasts forever, but if you are virtuous, you can stay in the present.

There are many types of pride which are unnecessary and will never bring you happiness.

Before there was the universe there was the natural law that allowed the universe to come into being, that is Tao.

To find balance we must be calm and detached as we allow ourselves to anchor lightly and naturally. The Tao tells us to go with the natural flow without attachment, yet we still need to be diligent as we take care of our day-to-day business.

Be true to who you are while remaining humble, with a child's mind full of potential as you walk the circle of life.

You cannot improve something that is perfect nor hold on too tightly to a flawless sphere or it will escape your grasp.

Avoid going to extremes without being complacent while staying in the middle.

If giving someone advise, remind them to take it easy, do not force something that does not fit but relax and let nature take its course for the best results.

Only use tools of force and destruction if there is no other way to preserve life and then do not celebrate your victory instead mourn for the fear that has been created.

The natural way is to flow, by attempting to harness a flow it must be divided which destroys that which we seek to use.

Knowing others and ourselves rather than mastering others and ourselves are two entirely different things. Knowing brings us wisdom and enlightenment while mastering requires the use of force and strength.

Through willpower, we persevere and are able to endure.

The Tao is great because it fulfills its purpose just by being.

To be in the presence of someone who follows the natural way brings peace.

In nature, we see that the soft can overcome the hard and that everything must be small before it can become large.

There must be room in order to receive.

Everywhere in nature, opposites are required.

The Tao does nothing but enables the universe.

If there were no desire the world would remain formless, tranquil and at peace.

Do not try to be good, just be good.
Do not try to accomplish something, just get the job done.
Do not force people, be kind and just.
Do not think too highly of yourself.
Do not get caught up with what appears on the surface but seek substance.

If you do not understand the reason behind a ritual then all that is left is a meaningless husk that will confuse.

The universe is complete.

The Tao is a circle that appears to flow downhill.

Life gives you what you put into it and what you are capable of understanding at the time.

For some what is hard is easy for others and what is easy is hard for others, so no worries the Tao will take care of everything.

You reap what you sow; by surrendering you will find the way.

Experience is the best teacher, by doing nothing but observing nature we learn the most.

What we see is that soft always overcomes hard.

Try to be content with what you have without attachment.

Once you attach to material things and do not attain them, you set yourself up for disappointment.

Try to find stillness and tranquility rather than seek to accomplish something that will eventually outlive its usefulness.

If you know what is enough you will always have enough.

The natural way is for peace and contentment.

The whole world is contained within ourselves. There is no need to look elsewhere for answers.

By trying to learn something, we are acquiring, by following the Tao we are letting go.

When you do nothing, there is nothing to do, that is the way of nature, it just takes its course.

Be concerned for others rather than yourself.

Be kind to others no matter what they have done.

There is nothing to fear but fear itself.

We are one with all things so why worry about death. If you do not worry about death it cannot grab hold of you.

The universe follows the Tao. It is formed from matter and fed from virtue but shaped by our environment.

The natural way requires no guidance.

To learn constancy look to the small for insight, and find your strength by yielding to force.

If you stop talking you can listen and fill your life.

It is hard not to be sidetracked from the path when you see some of the wonderful external objects that people accumulate. Those possessions are usually in excess and will not bring happiness.

If you look at the universe, you can see that by cultivating virtue in yourself you can help cultivate virtue in your family, community and even a nation. Fill yourself with virtue and seek harmony with nature. This is consistent with enlightenment and the way of the Tao.

The highest state of man is not to worry about what others think of you but to be humble and solve your problems as simply as possible.

Most people that talk too much do not know what they are talking about anyway.

Be just and do not strive to control people with restrictions or laws if you want to avoid poverty and theft.

By enjoying peace, people will become honest, if you have no desire than people can live a good and simple life.

Be straightforward but restrained; avoid severity rather lead with a light hand. If you are virtuous and use restraint when dealing with others you can provide a firm foundation for the Tao to take root and you will be serving heaven.

Use the Tao to approach everything and no matter how powerful the evil it will cause no harm.

If you wish to conquer, you must yield. By yielding, the larger absorbs the smaller.

The best gift you can give anyone is the gift of the Tao.

If you take problems too lightly they may wind up becoming even bigger problems later on, so take small steps instead of big ones, keep things simple and take care of the little things and you will never experience great difficulties.

Deal with potential problems before they happen, it is always easier to maintain than to try and repair. The whole dam can collapse from a little crack not taken care of properly.

If you hold onto a sponge filled with water too tightly you will squeeze out that which you are trying to hold onto, so stop trying to hold onto things and you will not lose them.

To understand the primal virtue of the natural way, try not to outsmart nature by attempting to be too clever. Lead by following and allow people to feel supported. Be humble and guide from behind rather than pulling or pushing. Do not compete with those you wish to guide. Be generous by being economical and courageous by being merciful, show humility you do not need to be ahead of everyone.

Do not be a violent soldier, nor an angry fighter, rather learn how to deal with people by not striving and being virtuous. Move without appearing to move, do without appearing to do. Do not be obvious in all things nor underestimate an opponent.

Most people never look below the surface where all the substance is.

It is easy to protect yourself by appearing uninteresting.

Even thought the natural way is very easy to follow most people cannot understand disciplined action.

Being healthy is when you are sick of being sick.

Be strong by understanding your ignorance. Know yourself but do not make a show of your knowledge. Be respectful of yourself but do not be arrogant. Keep a sense of awe in your life and leave other people alone. Even the wise man does not understand everything.
The people that do not think they are knowledgeable are the ones with knowledge.

The Tao is a plan that encompasses everything. All things are supplied and all problems solved.
The more you give to others the more you have.

The way of control is to threaten those that live in fear of dying with death. If you are not afraid of death, than you cannot be controlled by the threat of its loss.

When the rulers starve the people and demand too much life becomes less precious. When the people do not value their life, and the rulers interfere too much than the people will rebel.

Soft and yielding is the way of life and will overcome the hard and stiff, which is the way of death. The Tao is the way of balance in all things.

The great paradox of the Tao is that you get what you want.

Being yielding like water the weak can overcome the strong, yet the strong want to control and are allowed by the laws of nature to take control.

A man of virtue upholds his part of the bargain without expecting others to do the same. This is how to avoid resentment.

A small country does not need all the machines to provide for too many people. The people are content to live a simple life in peace with their neighbor.

Because words are beautiful does not make them the truth.

There is no effort for the way of nature just is.

Chapter 10 – Zen in the Martial Arts

Zen is a school of Mahāyāna Buddhism, which emphasizes a particularly form of experiential meditation, in the attainment of enlightenment. As such, it de-emphasizes theoretical knowledge in favor of direct, experiential realization through meditation and dharma practice. Zen asserts that all sentient beings have Buddha-nature, the universal nature of inherent wisdom and virtue, and emphasizes that Buddha-nature is nothing other than the nature of the mind itself. The aim of Zen practice is to discover this Buddha-nature within each person, through meditation and mindfulness of daily experiences. Zen practitioners believe that this provides new perspectives and insights on existence, which ultimately lead to enlightenment. The samurai found that much of their martial arts were just external forms. Once they found their physical body and external strength lacking, they sought to find ways to internalize their training. By training in Zen, the samurai were able to arrive at a state of no-mind bringing them back to their own original nature of wisdom and compassion.

The core of Zen practice is seated meditation known as Zazen, and recalls both the posture in which the Buddha is said to have achieved enlightenment under the Bodhi tree and the elements of mindfulness and concentration which are part of the Eightfold Path as taught by the Buddha. All of the Buddha's fundamental teachings—among them the Noble Eightfold Path, the Four Noble Truths, the idea of dependent origination, the five precepts, the five aggregates, and the three marks of existence—also make up important elements of the perspective that Zen takes for its practice.

The Ten Ox-herding Pictures

Another example of Zen teaching is the famous "Ox-herding Pictures." Our essential self is compared to an ox. The Ten Ox-herding Pictures have depicted the process in which the imperfect, limited, and relative self awakens to the perfect, unlimited, and absolute essential self, grasps it, tames it, forgets it, and completely incorporates it into the personality.

The author of the verses to the Ten Ox-herding Pictures, Master Kakuan Shion, was a disciple of Daizui Genjô [1065-1135], the twelfth in the line of Master Rinzai. His dates of birth and death as well as other information are unclear. To each of the ten pictures Master Kakuan has put a verse. I will give my own brief description along with what was originally written by Master Kakuan

Interpretation of the 10 Ox Herding Pictures

These paintings were done by Yokoo Tatsuhiko around 1800 in Japan.

Searching for the Ox
Incessantly you brush aside thick grasses in pursuit.
The waters are wide, the mountains far, and the path leads on without end.
Sapped of strength, exhausted in spirits, knowing no longer where to search.
You only hear the sound of the evening cicadas, chirping in the maple trees.

We are searching for something, but what is it that we are searching for? We travel farther and farther from our home because of our deluded senses. We are afraid because we desire to gain back what was lost of our own internal nature.

Seeing the Traces
At the water's edge, under the trees - hoofmarks are numerous.
Balmy grasses grow abundantly - can you see them or not?
Even if you go deeper and deeper into the mountains.
How could his nostrils, well compassing the heavens, hide him at all?

We are still confused as to what is true and what is false but we are starting to see traces. These traces are varied but suggest that what we see are reflections of our own self not the outside world.

Seeing the Ox
The bush warbler sings on the branch.
The sun is warm, the breeze gentle, and the willows on the riverbank are green.
There is no place you can escape from him.

We begin to see the origin of all things through our senses. When we are directed properly, we understand that is none other than ourselves that we seek.

Catching the Ox
You have exhausted all your faculties to take hold of him.
Because his spirit is strong and his strength abundant, it is difficult to rid him of his habits.
Sometimes he goes to the top of the high plain.
Other times he resides in clouds and smokes.

After many years of searching, we can finally grasp that of which we seek. However, how do we hold onto this realization when there is constant pressure from the outside world? We wish for harmony within ourselves but are not quite there yet. At times, we lose ourselves for brief periods.

Herding the Ox
Occasional whipping does not depart from the body.
Lest he follow his own whim, entering the dust and dirt.
If you devotedly tame him, he will be pure and gentle.
Without bridle and chains, he will follow you of his own accord.

Now is the time to hold on tightly. As we awaken, sleep may overtake us. How can we turn off the internal dialog and string of thoughts? Our mind is playing tricks on us. Only by letting go can we have what we want, but if we let go we may also lose our minds.

Coming Home on the Ox's Back
You mount the ox and want to make your way slowly home.
A barbarian plays the flute in the red glow of sunset.
Each measure, each tune is filled with ineffable tones.
Among true intimates, what need is there for words?

We are relaxed and at ease having surrendered. No more struggling to hold onto the illusion of gain or loss. There is no rush as we play a flute that is not there. Our hearts are filled with happiness.

The Ox Forgotten, Leaving the Man Alone
You have mounted the ox and already reached your home in the mountains.
The ox is gone and the person has nothing more to do.
Though the morning sun has already risen three bamboo lengths, he dreams on.
The whip and the halter, no longer of use, are hung up in the stall.

The symbolic ox is home and forgotten. We have found our way back and can sit serenely. We can sit-all day, dreaming because we no longer need to control that which is now ours.

The Ox and the Man Both Gone out of Sight
Whip, tether, person and ox - all are empty.
The blue sky spreads out far and wide, it cannot be communicated.
On a red-hot oven, how can there be any place for snow?
Having come this far, you understand the intention of the patriarchs.

We are no longer confused. We are no longer attached. We are full of emptiness. This is the spirit of Buddha without trying to follow.

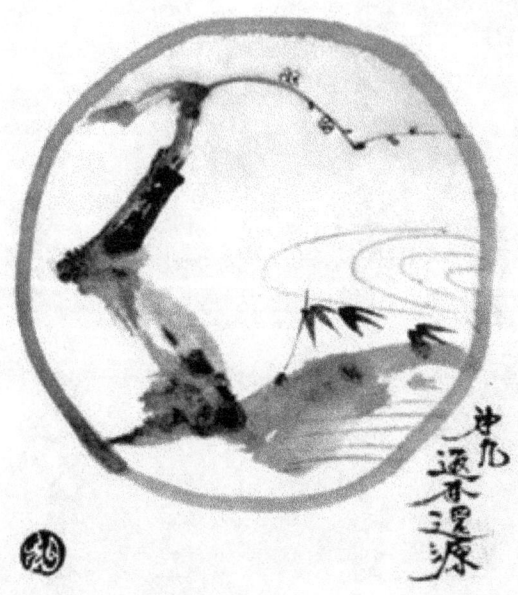

Returning to the Origin, Back to the Source
Having come back to the origin and returned to the source, you see that you have expended efforts in vain.
You are now back to your starting point. How much effort you needed for that! What could be superior to becoming blind and deaf in this very moment?
Inside the hermitage, you do not see what is in front of the hermitage. The water flows of itself and the flowers are naturally red.

We are now just an observer. No need to go anywhere or do anything. No need to think about what is going on in the external world. What is, is and what is not, is not.

Entering the City with Bliss-bestowing Hands
Shoeless and bare-chested he enters the marketplace.
He is daubed with earth and ashes, and a smile fills his face.
Making no use of the secrets of gods and wizards. He causes withered trees to bloom.

Nobody knows who you are as you look like a happy idiot. No need for the demonstration of power. Just allow those that seek the path to be touched by you and become Buddha.

Chapter 11 – Meditation for Warriors

Many forms of meditation may prove useful for the martial artist to access more of their human potential and become closer to reality. Through meditation, we can regain the ability to function more effectively and see how we are connected to the universe. Meditation brings me to a place where I feel like a person that is trying to remember something that I have forgotten. Although meditation can be a very hard discipline requiring hard work, it is not only the exercise itself that is important but also the result. Tuning and training the mind, just as the other aspects of Budo train the body, is one of the primary aims of all forms of meditation. By cleansing the gates of perception, we can comprehend reality, increase our serenity, and become more competent in our daily lives. There really is no endpoint to the possibilities of growth and development when you practice serious and disciplined meditation.

Meditation produces a physiological state of deep relaxation along with a heightened and alert mental state while lowering metabolism, heart rate, and respiration. The physiological state of this process is the opposite of what is brought on by anxiety or anger. The reason our body responds this way is that while in a meditative state we are focusing on doing one thing at a time. This mindfulness and being present are coherent and simple signals we can send to ourselves at any time in our daily life but made difficult in the now considered normal way in which we constantly multitask. We constantly live in memories of earlier on in our day or lives, as well as project into the future. No wonder we are mentally as well as physically drained. By allowing even a few minutes of meditation a day we can retreat into mindfulness and renew our mind and spirit while relieving tension.

There are many types of meditation. Sometimes described as "Poetry in Motion," because of its gentle, slow, and non-jarring movements. Tai Chi produces a high degree of relaxation and a balanced unification of body and mind while stretching and toning the body's muscles and circulating the internal healing energy. This form of moving meditation leaves you feeling alert, revitalized, yet relaxed with increased focus, harmony, and strength for your daily life. Other forms of this body-centered path would be Yoga or even dancing.

Other forms of meditation include quiet contemplation, where you would actively look, feel, and think about an object. This object can be physical or mental, but focused attention is of the utmost importance. The lack of discipline becomes quickly apparent when I tell my students to just think about the tip of their nose as they find themselves itching, twitching, and unable to concentrate for longer than a few seconds. Sometimes when focusing on an object such as a flame we start seeing illusions we project, or you feel yourself transform in size. The difficulty lies in trying not to get interested or involved with anything that will interfere with your concentration. Remember contemplation is a binding of the mind not the eye.

An easy way to start meditating is by counting the breath. This very structured form still allows us to do just one thing as completely as possible. Most beginning students start with a count of four or six and work their way up to slowing the breath to a count of up to 12 or more during the course of 10 to 20 minutes of this form of meditation and relaxation technique. Try not to hold the breath and decide if you are going to have your eyes open or shut as well as the duration before you start. Another related form is the counting of an imaginary object. You have all heard about counting sheep to help you relax and fall asleep. For thousands of years people have counted bubbles rising from the bottom of a lake or logs floating down a stream to reach this same state of structured mindfulness. Take these objects and put thoughts into them as you watch them pass by. Shift your attention to the next object coming. This technique is especially helpful if you are in a noisy environment. This technique is also useful while trying to meditate with background noise such as a dog barking or someone cutting their lawn. Sometimes you find just too many outside thoughts coming into your head to allow yourself to relax. Just take an irritation such as the neighbor's dog barking and turn it into a passing log or bubble. Your stress level will become much lower keeping you healthy and relaxed.

Other forms of meditation include the chanting of mantra and finger weaving mudra. These forms have a strong connection to some of the more esoteric studies of the martial arts and Buddhism. The Kuji-in which is sometimes referred to as the "Nine Hand Seals Technique", a specialized form of Buddhist meditation, derived from the Diamond Universe Nine Assemblies mandala of Shingon Buddhism. It is also used by other Buddhist sects, especially in Japan; some Taoists and practitioners of Shinto and Chinese traditional religion; and in folk-magic throughout East Asia. Kuji-in originated in India and was brought to Japan through the Buddhist movement. The modern version of Kuji-In technique is a contemplation of higher truth while in a deepened state of meditation. Originally the hand shapes were accompanied by Kuji-Kiri, The related practice of making nine cuts--five horizontal and four vertical, alternating--in the air or palm of a hand with the finger or on paper with a brush. There are as many as 81 variations of the Kuji-in within certain sects of Buddhism in Japan. There are also many other mudra that are used in the world. The Kuji-in are steeped in esoteric Buddhist beliefs, especially Mikkyo. The Kuji-in are used in a number of their meditations, both those related simply to their religious practice and those dealing with their martial arts.

Meditation is part of the human experience and commonplace. We may not even be aware of the nuances or variations that acquire when we concentrate, calm ourselves, or regain our composure. When we experience excitement or rapture, increase our energy and alertness we are experiencing unconscious factors of the meditative process. We have all had the experience of being entirely captivated by something where our awareness becomes focused, and time perception is altered. Most of us have had to take a deep breath and regain our composure seeking to calm ourselves down after an interpersonal confrontation or our buttons get pushed. When we look inside to investigate our daily experiences hidden secrets will be revealed, and with a little faith, we can learn and become better people. As it was said by Socrates, "The un examined life is not worth living."

Chapter 12 - Conclusion

The concern with perfection is a mistake. It is better for students of the martial arts to embody the curiosity, feeling, and innocence of a child. Try to develop a talent for imperfection. At some point, many martial artists stop training and start teaching. Their understanding of Budo stagnates and their ego has trapped them from ever making the inner progress let alone improvement towards better Taijutsu. Another trap awaits students who have never developed the fundamentals through years of training in the basics and instead try to imitate the master teachers.

There are many resources available today that were not around when I was starting my journey. The internet, YouTube, and vast quantities of books on technique are staggering. Unfortunately, there is no short cut to hard work. Having a bookmark to a technique on YouTube that you can watch or a book with hundreds of pictures and explanations of how to do Kata and technique only makes you a collector of such information. A notebook, video, or book is only for reference not a replacement to taking class and practicing on your own. There is not replacement for practice and reflection or the use during live combat. I have many students who like to remind me of the other ways they have learned to do a particular technique. But I would much rather have a student who always feels like they are never going to get good, and every time they see me repeat or refine what they are learning, find something that they had never noticed before. So again, perseverance, and the talent for imperfection along with attitude of playing and enjoying the process makes for a better student of Budo. The wisdom of insecurity is not an evasion, but a way of carrying on and continuing to learn and grow your martial arts. To interpret the words of Lao Tzu, be subtle, mysterious, profound, and responsive. Be watchful as if crossing a winter stream and alert like men aware of danger. Yielding like ice about to melt, simple like an un-carved block of wood and hollow like a cave. Remain still until the movement of action is needed and do not be swayed by the desire for change. Know the strength of man but keep a woman's care. Be the stream of the universe ever true and unswerving. Become as a little child once more.

We live in a modern world of phones and computers, the Internet and buildings of steel and glass. In some ways, it is much more difficult to achieve spiritual balance than in the old days of isolated villages. As Somerset Maughn wrote in his book the Razors Edge, "It is much easier to be a holy man on the mountain." Our challenge is to find and integrate the spiritual aspects of Budo as well as the physical transformations that occur naturally by years of practice and hard work. Even physical transformations are misunderstood in this modern world, to exclude the thinking center of the body. It is the body that becomes activated through slow meditative practice and awareness, not the brain.

There are infinite ways of negotiating both living and dying. Although we talk about killing an opponent's fighting spirit not just their balance, what we are really learning is how to take away their heart or desire to fight. First off, all possible conditions are nothing but phenomena, which are transitory. Because of a yearning for sensation there is cause for phenomena, which psychologically speaking, is nothing more than a prolonged dream state filled with hallucinatory visions that result from our mental content and karma. Once we realize the unreality of existence then we are free to control our thinking process so we can concentrate the mind in an effort to reach right knowledge. There are no external opponents, adversaries, or deities. There is nothing apart from ourselves. We are one with all that is.

References

Wile, D (1983), Yang Family Secret Transmissions. New York: Sweet Ch'I Press

Sohl, R and Carr, A (1976), Games Zen Masters Play. New York: Signet

Jou, Tsung Hwa, (1984), The Tao of I Ching. Taiwan: Tai Chi Foundation

Jou, Tsung Hwa, (1983), The Tao of Meditation. New York: Tai Chi Foundation

Poliakoff, M (1987), Combat Sports In The Ancient World. New Haven: Yale University Press

LeShan, L (1974), How To Meditate. Boston: Bantam Books

Watts, A (1951), The Wisdom of Insecurity. New York: Vintage Books

Epstein, P (2001), Kabbalah, The Way of the Jewish Mystic. Boston: Shambhala

English, J (1997), Tao Te Ching. New York: Vintage Books

Hatsumi, M (1980) Togakure Ryu Ninpo Taijutsu. Tokyo: Kodansha

Pariyatti (1984) Noble Eightfold Path: Way to the End of Suffering. New York: Buddhist Publication Society

www.ingramcontent.com/pod-product-compliance
Lightning Source LLC
LaVergne TN
LVHW041458070426
835507LV00009B/680